WORLD SERIES CHAMPIONS

PHILADELPHIA PHILLIES

Published by Creative Education
P.O. Box 227, Mankato, Minnesota 56002
Creative Education is an imprint of The Creative Company
www.thecreativecompany.us

Design and production by Blue Design
Printed by Corporate Graphics in the United States of America

Photographs by Corbis (Bettmann, Duomo), Getty Images (Altrendo Travel, Diamond Images, Focus on Sport, Jesse D. Garrabrant, Jeff Gross, Hulton Archive, Paul Jaslenski, Mitchell Layton, Robert Leiter/MLB Photos, Jim McIsaac, Ronald C. Modra/Sports Imagery, National Baseball Hall of Fame Library/MLB Photos, Photo File/MLB Photos, Rich Pilling/MLB Photos, Louis Requena/ MLB Photos, George Silk//Time Life Pictures, Tony Tomsic/MLB Photos, Ron Vesely/MLB Photos)

Library of Congress Cataloging-in-Publication Data

Frisch, Aaron.
Philadelphia Phillies / by Aaron Frisch.
p. cm. — (World Series champions)
Includes index.
ISBN 978-1-58341-693-8
1. Philadelphia Phillies (Baseball team)—History—Juvenile literature. I. Title. II. Series.

GV875.P45F75 2009
796.357'640974811—dc22   2008003766

CPSIA: 100109 PO1081

9 8 7 6 5 4 3 2

Cover: Second baseman Chase Utley (top), 1980 Phillies (bottom)
Page 1: Shortstop Jimmy Rollins
Page 3: Outfielder Bobby Abreu

WORLD SERIES CHAMPIONS
PHILADELPHIA PHILLIES

AARON FRISCH

CREATIVE EDUCATION

The Phillies are a team in **Major League Baseball**. They play in Philadelphia, Pennsylvania. Philadelphia was a very important city when America first became a country.

ST. LOUIS
\# 22 ECKSTEIN   SS
43 ENCARNACIO RF
5 PUJOLS   1B
15 EDMONDS   CF
27 ROLEN   3B
99 TAGUCHI   LF
4 MOLINA   C
12 MILES   2B
29 CARPENTER   P
\# 29 CARPENTER

                 1 2 3
ST. LOUIS   1 0
PHILLIES   0 0 1

6

Citizens Bank Park

The Phillies' stadium is called Citizens Bank Park. Their uniforms are red, white, and gray. The Phillies play lots of games against teams called the Braves, Marlins, Mets, and Nationals.

PITCHER
GROVER CLEVELAND ALEXANDER

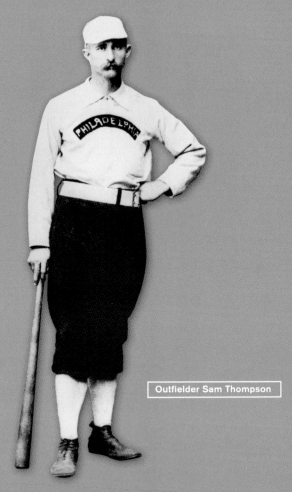

Outfielder Sam Thompson

The Phillies played their first
season in 1883. Their first
star player was outfielder
Sam Thompson. He could hit
the ball hard. The Phillies got
to the World Series in 1915.
But they lost.

Pitcher Robin Roberts

OUTFIELDER
CY WILLIAMS

After that, the Phillies had lots of good hitters like outfielder Cy Williams. But they still lost a lot of games. Philadelphia got a great pitcher named Robin Roberts in 1948. He helped the Phillies get to the World Series in 1950. But they lost again.

ll

PITCHER
STEVE CARLTON

12

THIRD BASEMAN
MIKE SCHMIDT

In 1972, the Phillies got
two good players. Steve
Carlton was a pitcher. He
won the **Cy Young Award**
four times. Mike Schmidt
was a third baseman. He
hit lots of home runs.

BOB BOONE

The Phillies got to the **playoffs** in 1976, 1977, and 1978. In 1980, the Phillies got to the World Series. They beat a team called the Royals. The Phillies were world champions for the first time!

GREG LUZINSKI

15

DARREN DAULTON

The Phillies played in the World Series again in 1983. But this time they lost. They got new stars like Lenny Dykstra after that. Dykstra was an outfielder who always **hustled**. He helped Philadelphia get to the World Series in 1993. But the Phillies lost again.

OUTFIELDER
LENNY DYKSTRA

17

FIRST BASEMAN
JIM THOME

19

SHORTSTOP
JIMMY ROLLINS

Philadelphia fans got to watch some exciting new players in the seasons after that. Jimmy Rollins was a quick shortstop who was good at stealing bases. Once, he got a hit in 38 straight games.

First baseman Ryan Howard was another good player. In 2008, he hit two home runs in the World Series to help the Phillies beat the Tampa Bay Rays to become champions again. Philadelphia fans hope that today's Phillies will win another World Series soon!

GLOSSARY

Cy Young Award — an award that is given to the best pitcher in the league

hustled — played with lots of energy

Major League Baseball — a group of 30 baseball teams that play against each other; major-league teams have the best players in the world

playoffs — games that are played after the season to see which team is the champion

PHILLIES FACTS

Team colors: red, white, and gray

First home stadium: Recreation Park

Home stadium today: Citizens Bank Park

League/Division: National League, Eastern Division

First season: 1883

World Series championships: 1980, 2008

Team name: The Phillies got their name because of where they play. Sometimes people call Philadelphia "Philly" for short. A person from Philadelphia can be called a "Philly," too.

Major League Baseball Web site for kids:
http://www.mlb.com/mlb/kids/

INDEX